MIXED COMPANY

CARTOONS

BY

MICHAEL MASLIN

A FIRESIDE BOOK
PUBLISHED BY SIMON & SCHUSTER INC.
NEW YORK LONDON TORONTO SYDNEY TOKYO SINGAPORE

Fireside
Simon & Schuster Building
Rockefeller Center
1230 Avenue of the Americas
New York, New York 10020

Manufactured in the United States of America

10 9 8 7 6 5 4 3 2 1 Pbk.

Library of Congress Cataloging in Publication Data

Maslin, Michael.
    Mixed company: cartoons / by Michael Maslin.
        p.   cm.
    "A Fireside book."
    I. Title.
  NC1429.M4247A4   1990
  741.5'973—dc20

90-33528
CIP

ISBN 0-671-66338-0 Pbk.

To Lee Lorenz

"We'll begin, Mr. Bergeron, just as soon as you're seated."

"I've taken him back, but I haven't taken him in."

"*Sorry, but I'm going to have to issue you a summons for reckless grammar and driving without an apostrophe.*"

"Lately he's been spending more and more of his time with bell peppers and less and less of his time with me."

"*Ladies and gentlemen, the chicken, and,
in a related development, the egg.*"

"*You talk a lot about the need for more popcorn,
but I don't see you doing anything about it.*"

7

"*I wish to voice a complaint.*"

9

"It's spring, sir. May I take your hat and coat?"

"No calls for the rest of the day, Miss Bromley—
I'll be carving my pumpkin."

11

"And _your_ problems will always be _my_ problems, Wendy—
except when I'm really, really busy."

"*This is Chet—friend, confidant, dog.*"

13

FALL GUYS

"I suggest you speak with my husband—he makes all the deliveries."

"If the past is any indication of the future, he'll have a cruller."

17

"*Look around, Dennis. Do you see room for a marriage?*"

"Shall we?"

"*I've never been surer of anything in my life, Pamela—one stuffed pepper will be enough for the two of us.*"

"*I have some good news, Mr. and Mrs. Montly.
Your drive shaft is going to be all right.*"

"This trial is about more than just a bagel and cream cheese. This trial is about a bagel and cream cheese with chives."

"*Does it have to be a walk? Couldn't we go for a drive?*"

"I'm afraid there is no more up, sir—there is only down."

"*Your Majesty.*"

"From Hollywood, the 'Tonight Show,' starring Johnny Carson."

"You've played hopscotch before."

"*Have you been here since I put everything on casters?*"

"It was not its usual self this morning. It was unresponsive and sluggish. I put my hand on its hood and it felt very, very hot. That's when I decided to call you."

"*Would everyone check to see they have an attorney? I seem to have ended up with two.*"

"Move 'em out!"

"The sun's down, and the moon and stars are out.
Will there be anything else, sir?"

"*Beware of the dog.*"

"I don't ever want this moment to end, Darla,
but someone's got to stir the tortellini."

"Why don't you take a seat, and I'll see if I can pry him away from his desk."

"*Until the morning news then, good night.*"

"*A prawn—Hunan style—for your thoughts.*"

"*Tuesday night is Tympani Night.*"

"I don't want you to go for a walk because *I* want you to go for a walk. I want you to go for a walk because *you* want to go for a walk."

"Let's do more than just repaint—let's marbleize."

"*Yes, I've seen it before. It's a double-dip, double-Dutch-chocolate ice-cream cone. I recognize the sprinkles.*"

43

"*This concludes the conscious part of your day. Good night.*"

"*If we have inconvenienced you by neglecting to fork-split your English muffin this morning, we are truly, truly sorry.*"

"I can't pinpoint it exactly, but sometime during our twenty-third year of marriage Wesley began taking notes."

"*Soon you will be given an inch. You will take a mile.*"

"*Your transmission specialists—Ed, Rudy, Phil, and Bob.*"

"Here comes the King Crab."

SHOP AND MOP

"Here to see you on official business, the state bird of New Jersey—the eastern goldfinch."

"*Jeff, I'm going to need some time to prepare a counterproposal.*"

"*You look like you could use another scoop of mint chocolate chip.*"

"*Your favorite sweater isn't here. I sent it out to be cleaned and carbon-dated.*"

"Mr. Huffington, the voice of Mrs. Huffington."

"May I speak with the dog of the house?"

"It has been my long-standing policy to neither confirm nor deny the
Mother Goose stories you've been hearing."

THE OLD MAN AND THE SEA AND THE
OLD MAN'S PORTABLE COLOR TV

"*I would like what's left of the missing box of chocolate-covered graham crackers returned to the kitchen table as soon as possible. There will be no questions asked.*"

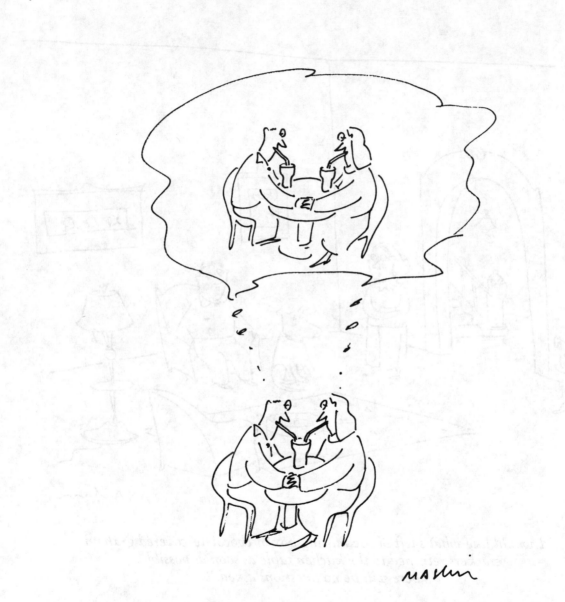

"*Mr. Kearn has stepped out of character for the afternoon. May I take a message?*"

"Please note, today is the last day I will say 'Have a nice day' to you. Starting tomorrow, I will say 'Have a good one.'"

"The jury's still out on your cheese balls."

"Is Margie's Yule Log getting bigger every year, or are
we getting smaller?"

"*Strike that whinny.*"

"*While I do represent your disgruntled employees, Mr. Hollingwood,*
I am not a disgruntled employee myself."

"*Apparently they're going to stick to their story of love at first sight.*"

"*That was your father speaking. Now hear this—
this is your <u>mother</u> speaking.*"

"Howard usually shrinks from meeting new people."

"*Trouble, Edna. The bees are chirping and the birds are buzzing.*"

"Papa Bear, Mama Bear, Baby Bear, and Me"

"Bottleneck Ho!"

"And the lighting. Candle, incandescent, neon, or house?"

"My critics are few, but outspoken."

"*Your application says you're a trained bear. Can you be more specific?*"

"Gee, Kevin, I don't know what to say. No one's ever told me I had tongue-and-groove flooring before."

"*The man I thought I married never materialized.*"

"*I'll have a quarter pound of your most reliable cheese.*"

"He'll be back right after the street lights are turned on."

FROM SNOWBALL TO SNOWMAN
the autobiography of FROSTY
MASLIN

MANAGER
OF THE
MONTH

90

"*See you tonight around six, unless, of course, I run into overtime.*"

"*I'm late, you're angry—we quarrel.*"

"*Well—I don't think I have to tell you gentlemen when we've reached a foregone conclusion.*"

"*You have a very large mouse problem.*"

"*Case in point.*"

"*I like a man who can make me laugh.*"

RESORT COURT

"*May I suggest a wine to go with your spat?*"

"I'm at a secret training camp somewhere in the foothills of Connecticut.
Behind me—food and soft drink specialists, marching off to join the
Hamburger War."

"*I'm sorry, but our copy of Self and Future Self was just checked out.*"

"On second thought, I'll have sangria. I had rosé
the last time we buried the hatchet."

"I mean it Frank. I'm going now—that is, unless you tell me to stay."

"It was written as a gripping story of a man and his dog battling the elements, but with some tinkering, I suppose it _could_ be a screwball comedy."

"*Did we come here to talk, or did we come here to snorkle?*"

"*The first time I saw her, she was drinking sugar-free, salt-free, caffeine-free cream soda. I was drinking my usual brand of cola. We had nothing in common, really, except carbonation.*"

SEAL APPEAL

"*Depending on who you talk to, he either quit or was fired.*"

"I could double-check, sir, but I believe the last of the
coconut frozen-fruit bars now rests in your hand."

"*The torch? It's for Karen Ackerhill—his high school sweetheart.*"

"Will Allen B. Brussel please come forward? New Jersey, the Garden
State, has a bone to pick with you."

"*I'll get the drinks—you get their coats.*"

"*I believe we finally have something for you to put in writing.*"

LAW AND ORDER

"*Marvin, do you realize that if you continue to set the record straight about each and every little thing, then that's all we'll ever have time for?*"

WRITE OR PHONE
AHEAD

119

SUMMER DRIVING'S NOT SO GRUELING WHEN YOU'RE CAR POOLING

"You'll _have_ to wear this, George—your monkey suit is still at the cleaner's."

GHOSTS OF GAS PRICES PAST

"If you don't mind, I'd like to have all of this in writing."

"This court, featuring the unique judicial stylings of the Honorable Jay Rallwell, is now in session."

SOMETHING THE CAT DRAGGED IN

"*Just when I'm thinking you've run out of surprises you tell me Gouda is your favorite cheese.*"

127

"We invited ourselves; didn't you get the invitation?"

"*What sounded like a pigeon cooing in your backseat was a pigeon cooing in your backseat.*"

"If you're going to put everything in its proper
perspective, I'll have another espresso."

"*Something, perhaps, in a best-seller?*"

WHILE SHE READ SHE CRIED, AND AS SHE
CRIED, HER CHICKEN — KENTUCKY STYLE — FRIED.

"Say 'hello' to leather, say 'good-bye' to chintz."

"*Ladies and gentlemen, the cheerleaders to the President
of the United States.*"

"*Now that we've been introduced, Mr. Kelvey, I'd like to bring an old friend of mine—the interrogative sentence—into our conversation.*"

"*I'll be sitting to Ed's right; Jeff, you'll sit directly across from him; and, Lois, you'll be to his left.*"

TRADITION · COMPETITION · TUITION

139

"The truth, Harriet—which are you happier to see: me or the cherries jubilee?"

"*I'm afraid we'll need more time to fight for the check.*"

"It's not the heat. It's not the humidity. It's the Haroldsons."

"*How did it go today? And, if I may, I'd like a follow-up.*"

PERRY B. PAUL STOPS TO POP HIS TOP AFTER SEEING A RAINDROP

"*We didn't order any encyclopedias.*"

THE DOOR-TO-DOOR SYMPHONY

"They're offering a deal—you pay court costs and damages, they drop charges of breaking and entering."

"If I may, Mr. Perlmutter, I'd like to answer your question <u>with</u> a question."

"*I'm sorry, Neil. I underestimated you.*"

ABOUT THE AUTHOR

Michael Maslin is a cartoonist for *The New Yorker* magazine. He lives in New York with his wife, Liza Donnelly, an artist and writer, and their daughter, Ella. He has published three other cartoon collections, *The More the Merrier, The Gang's All Here!* and *The Crowd Goes Wild.*